HISTORY OF THE SCOTTISH FOLD

For some cat breeds, their history of development goes back many centuries; their origins are lost in unrecorded times and places. These are the breeds that the cat fancy refers to as "natural." This is somewhat of an exaggeration because prior to the establishment of organized cat century to create a pool of breeds. From them, other breeds have been produced by hybridization. Additionally, a few other breeds have been developed from natural mutations that spontaneously occur in all animals from time to time. The Scottish Fold is one such breed.

The Scottish Fold occurred as a spontaneous mutation on a farm in Perthshire, Scotland, in 1961. The mutation causes the ears to fold down in a semi-pendulous manner. Owner, Terry Havel.

shows and the recording of pedigrees during the later years of the 19th century, cats existed only as basic "types," rather than specific breeds.

These basic types were refined during the early years of the 20th A mutation is a change in the way one or more genes express themselves. Thereafter, they act in a predictable manner and can either be retained and propagated in a population, or specifically bred to remove their occurrence.

Some mutations affect the color of an animal, some the hair length or other anatomical feature.

Examples in cats are the taillessness in the Manx and Japanese Bobtail, long hair in the Persian and many other breeds, lack of hair in the Sphynx, outward ear curling in the American Curl, and colors such as blue, lilac, and others, which are dilutions of normal wild-type colors. The pattern of the Siamese, together with various color shading patterns, are further mutations that have been retained to widen the choice of colors and features to create an ever-growing list of breeds.

In the Scottish Fold, the mutation affects the ears, causing the tips to fold down in a semi-pendulous manner. Unfortunately, to complete your understanding of mutations, that which is deemed fashionable and worthy of retention may also be inherently linked with genetic anatomical or physiological maladies. Such is the case with the genes that create the Scottish Fold, the Manx, and the Sphynx, as three examples.

It is essential that any potential breeder clearly understands the genetic negatives associated with the Fold. If he does not, these qualities may manifest themselves in the offspring that are produced. Essentially, the Scottish Fold, as a breed, is a hybrid at every generation. This means that when Folds are mated, they must be paired only to cats that are *not* Scottish Folds. We will discuss the matter again later.

SUSIE—THE MOTHER OF THE BREED

In 1961 in a farmyard in Perthshire, Scotland, a Mr. William Ross noticed an unusual cat. Her name was Susie. She was of unknown origin, was white, and displayed folded ears and a rather short and thickened tail. Ross asked the owner if he could obtain one of any kittens that she had that displayed the folded ears, which he quickly realized was a rather unique feature.

Two years later, he and his wife Mollie were able to acquire one of the two Folds that Susie produced. She was named Denisla Snooks. Denisla was paired to a red tabby, and, from this union, one male Fold, called Snowball, was born. He was mated to a British Shorthair called Lady May. This pairing yielded five Folds. Among them was another white male, which was named Denisla Snowdrift.

Denisla Snooks was paired to another shorthair named Rylands Regal Gent, and this resulted in Denisla Hester of Mini and Denisla Hector. The other four Folds resulting from the Snowball ex Lady May litter seem not to have been recorded in literature, so whether or not they were productively bred or sold as pets remains unknown.

Denisla Hester of Mini was imported to the US by Lyn Lamoureux, who became a major figure, along with a number of other breeders, in promoting the Fold in America. Hester was leased to other breeders, and so from the Denisla lineage the Scottish Fold was developed.

The Scottish Fold is a friendly cat with an even disposition. Silver mackerel tabby owned by Sandy Greenbaum.

Two-month-old male Fold kitten.

THE OUTCROSS BREEDS

Because of the necessity to mate a Fold to a non-Fold, the breed has not suffered the negative consequences of inbreeding that sometimes happens when the gene pool of a newly developing breed is small. You have seen that in Britain the Fold was originally mated to British Shorthairs. This ensured a mixed (heterogeneous) genotype. When the breed arrived in the US, it was mated with American Shorthairs, as well as with Exotic Shorthairs and possibly other shorthaired breeds.

The theory in the early days was exactly the same as it is today. That is, a Fold should be mated only to the fittest and healthiest examples of the chosen outcross. Today, the only allowable outcross breeds accepted by the CFA (Cat Fanciers' Association), the largest of the American registries, are the British and American Shorthairs. These two breeds are also the choice for other registries that accept the Fold for registration.

The first Scottish Fold registered with the CFA was Wyola Jed Callant, who was the result of a mating between the imported Denisla Hestor of Mini to a black Exotic Shorthair called Leprechaun's Hurst of Wyola. Susie, the original Scottish Fold, was among the first Folds to be on the acceptance list of the CFA.

THE BREED GAINS AMERICAN POPULARITY

Once a new breed is initially accepted as a breed by a major cat registry, this gives it considerable help in gaining popularity. In 1974, the CFA granted the Fold experimental status. In 1976, it became possible to register the breed. It was upgraded in 1977 from experimental to provisional status.

In order to further promote the breed, Mrs Salle Peters, who was one of the breeders who leased Denisla Hestor of Mini, together with William and Mollie Ross, the founders of the breed, formed the International Scottish Fold Association. This was around 1974.

The result of these events was that the Scottish Fold became the subject of much media interest, and of course the cat magazines added extra impetus with their articles on the breed. At American cat shows, the Fold always commanded considerable interest from a public eager to obtain a new cat breed that really was very different from any other feline in its appearance.

In the decade 1978-1988, Fold registrations rose with every passing year. Of the 36 breeds that were accepted for registration with the CFA during the same period, the *only* other breed that could make such a claim was, ironically, the British Shorthair. By the end of that ten-year-period, the Fold had risen from obscurity to become the ninth most popular cat registered with the CFA. It was ahead of such well-known breeds as the Birman, the Rex breeds, British Shorthair, Russian Blue, Manx, Angora,

Korat, and Somali, to name but a few. By 1995, the Fold more than doubled its 1988 registrations and had risen to 6th place in CFA popularity, a considerable achievement. It is unlikely that it can improve much on this because the breeds ahead of it include such stalwarts as the Persian, Siamese, Maine Coon, Abyssinian, and Burmese.

associations, wanted nothing to do with this new mutation- based breed.

Their reasoning was based on the negative side effects that are linked to the Fold's flop-eared carriage. Europeans in general, and the British in particular, take very conservative stands on what is, and is not, acceptable in cat-breeding circles. It was considered

Brown tabby Longhair Scottish Fold owned by JoAnn Hinkle.

REJECTION IN EUROPE

While Americans readily embraced the Scottish Fold as a welcome addition to the list of cat breeds from which they could choose, Europeans took a different viewpoint. The Governing Council of the Cat Fancy (GCCF), Britain's major, and the world's oldest, cat registry, together with most other European cat

that the negative consequences related to the breeding of the Fold far outweighed any benefits that the breed had to offer. This same situation also applies to the Sphynx, an almost hairless cat, and any other breed that has negative health associations linked to it.

At this point it should be stated that the Manx is also based on a

The unusual appearance of a Scottish Fold's ears are created by folds in the outer rim of the ear that make the ear tips bend forward. Red tabby and white owned by Noni Ehrola.

The color varieties of the Scottish Fold include blue, red, white, black, cream, chinchillas, smokes, tabbies, patched, and bi-colors.

negative mutation but is accepted as a breed in its British homeland, and other countries, on the historical grounds that it was established and accepted as a breed from the time when the cat fancy first started in the 19th century. In light of its genetic base, this hardly seems a justifiable reason today if other comparable breeds are to be rejected, but that is the position. However, in Germany the Manx is now subject to bans in some areas, and this stance may spread to other countries in due course.

This does not mean that the Scottish Fold is not seen in Britain and Europe, where it has a dedicated following. It means that it cannot be exhibited and registered with many of the large associations. It will never become the popular breed that it is in the US, where most of its development has, as a result, taken place, unless there is a change in viewpoint, which seems unlikely.

The Fold is, however, gaining popularity as a show cat in Japan and is now also found in Russia. In both Sweden and Italy, the breed is arousing great interest, and some Folds are being exhibited in associations that accept the breed.

SO WHAT ARE THE PROBLEMS?

Although this chapter is devoted specifically to the history of the Scottish Fold, the negatives associated with the breed have influenced its development and acceptance, or lack of it, in many countries. It is therefore appropriate that these matters are discussed so that you have a full and balanced view of the breed when deciding if it is suited to your particular needs.

Without delving into the subject of genetics, it can be said that a cat inherits half of its genes from one parent and half from the other. Where the gene that determines folded ears is concerned, if *both* parents pass this gene to their offspring, there is the strong possibility that the kitten will develop a short, thick tail.

The cartilage in the legs also becomes thickened and can result in lameness, or an inability to walk at all. The feet also swell.

If, however, only *one* of the parents pass the fold gene to the offspring, the negative anomalies described are either not apparent or are in a very mild form that does not seem to affect the general health of the cat. It walks and runs like any other feline.

This is the reason why two Folds should *never* be mated because this would, of course, create the double-gene situation discussed. Fortunately, the fold-ear gene is semi-dominant. This means that it cannot be passed unseen to the cat population as a whole. If a cat has inherited the gene, it will be displayed via the folded ears, the degree of fold being individually variable in the breed.

This is where breeder/owner obligations are very important to potential Scottish Fold owners. Those obtaining a Fold as a pet should ensure that it is neutered

Scottish Fold littermates. Owner, Donna McDonald.

(male) or spayed (female) as soon as it is old enough. This removes any possibility that the gene could be passed into the "street cat" population, where it *could* double up via uncontrolled breeding. A desexed cat is still eligible for exhibition in what are called the altered cat classes.

A breeder should ensure that his Folds are never at liberty to mate with the local cats of the neighborhood, and, of course, that they are mated *only* to non-Fold cats of the designated breeds of British or American Shorthairs. If pet owners and breeders do not maintain the moral code required by the breed, it will almost certainly be the ruination of Scottish Folds, at least from the high-popularity standpoint. Fortunately, to this point in time, owners have shown responsibility.

THE LONGHAIR SCOTTISH FOLD

When a new shorthaired breed arrives on the scene, it is usually only a question of time before a longhaired version is produced.

During the 1980s, this happened in the Scottish Fold, although some Longhair Scottish Folds were believed to have existed almost from the time that immediately followed the mutation's first appearance.

Long hair arrives in a breed either through natural mutation or by crossing to a longhaired breed. In the case of the Fold, it is via crossing to a longhaired breed, or through a longhaired-gene carrier.

Logically, the most expedient route to take is to a visibly

longhaired cat, such as a Persian, or even an Exotic Shorthair, which itself is the creation of a British or American Shorthair crossed to a Persian.

Such a mating guarantees that all the resulting litter will carry the longhaired gene. If any of the litter are also Folds, the pairing of them to a longhaired breed will result in all longhaired kittens, with the theoretical expectation that half of them will also be Folds. It should be added that the kittens *not* displaying the folded ears do *not* carry the fold-ear gene at all in their makeup: they are totally normal cats, a fact that even people in the breed do not always understand.

Of course, in obtaining Longhair Scottish Folds, the breed cannot be paired with the recommended British or American Shorthairs, so you will appreciate that the Scottish Fold is unusual not only in its appearance but also in the way it is bred.

The Longhair Scottish Fold has proven to be a popular variety. It is also unusual in the cat fancy because the longhaired variety is still called a Scottish Fold. More commonly, when a longhaired variety of a shorthaired breed is created, it is given a totally different breed name. The Siamese, Abyssinian, Manx, and Russian Blue in their longhaired varieties respectively become the breeds of Balinese, Somali, Cymric, and Nebelung.

There was a move within the fancy to call the Longhair Scottish Fold the Highland Fold, but this was resisted by the major

The eyes should be wide open with a sweet expression. Owner, Michael E. Nelson.

American registries. Some breeders do, however, advertise longhaired kittens as Highland Folds.

SUCCESS AGAINST THE ODDS

The Scottish Fold's appearance and lovable charm have enabled it to do something extremely rare in the cat fancy: it has overcome all of the theoretical odds against it ever gaining any sort of popularity. America is the most liberal country in the world for accepting new breeds of any domestic animal, regardless of whether or not they have known negatives associated with them.

However, even Americans are not that liberal or, put another way, do apply a great deal of common sense to what they support.

Sometimes this is misunderstood outside of this nation. Put into plain English, any oddball variety of an animal has the *opportunity* to gain recognition in the US that it might not gain elsewhere so readily, if at all. But, unless that oddball animal really does have something to offer, it will never achieve more than a brief moment of success. It will soon enough be relegated to the ranks of a rare variety, which is what it would be in most other countries.

The Scottish Fold has run the gauntlet of criticism even in the US, yet it has survived to become one of the most popular cat breeds in America. The breed has proven that with responsible owner and breeder management, it is no more of a problem than the button-nosed Persian or the Manx. It has proven itself to be a feline loved by many thousands of people. Its devotees are spreading around the world, and, thirty-five years after the fold ears first appeared in Susie, it is showing no signs of slowing down.

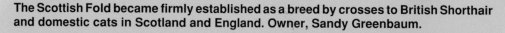

The Scottish Fold became firmly established as a breed by crosses to British Shorthair and domestic cats in Scotland and England. Owner, Sandy Greenbaum.

CHARACTER OF THE SCOTTISH FOLD

The Scottish Fold has a character that embraces the very best of temperament from its principle ancestors—the American and British Shorthairs, plus a special something that seems to emanate from the genetic mutation that creates the folded ears.

Of course, there is no evidence to prove that the mutation has any bearing whatsoever on the character of the Fold. Yet these cats seemingly display a special charm. Maybe this is just something that their owners alone see within the breed and that may be linked more to the unusual appearance of the breed's head, and the expression it creates. Be this as it may, if you talk with any Scottish Fold owner, they will assure you that this breed is like no other.

CHARMINGLY GENTLE

To be truly characteristic of the breed, a Fold, above all else, should be both charming and gentle with humans. Sometimes the Fold can *appear* to be less than friendly if it has short ears that lie very close to the head. People not aware of this anatomical anomaly may think that it is depressing its ears like the average angry feline. But this is not the case, unless of course it really is angry, in which case you will be left in no doubts on that account!

The ears can, in fact, suggest a whole range of emotional states, such as startled, curious, and cute. But these you must become familiar with to know they are normal. You then quickly see the true charm of the breed. The Fold is a cat that basically enjoys being relaxed. It gets on with just about any one—adults, children, other cats, and other pets. This makes for an easy life.

Historically, the British and American Shorthairs were developed from a long line of felines that needed to be very tough just to survive the lives most of them lived. They learned to live in harmony with their environment, and this blessed them with their stoic nature. This does not mean they are unemotional, more that they appear reserved and austere, seeing no need to bowl you over with overt affection. Rather, they display gentle affection that is consistent, never momentary. Their charm is inherent. It takes little time for them to win over people who have never been fortunate enough to be previously acquainted with them.

AN INTELLIGENT FELINE

The Fold is a very intelligent cat. This is not displayed in the same exuberant way as that of the Siamese, or other cats of foreign type, but more in the common

The body of the Scottish Fold is medium, rounded, and even from shoulder to pelvic girdle. Owner, Donna McDonald.

sense sort of way that you would expect of a street-smart feline. There is, to use a modern idiom, a "done it, been there, seen it" sort of attitude in the Scottish Fold's view of its world. It sees no need to impress you with its intelligence. But, during its day-to-day life, you will become acutely aware that its gray matter evolved to enable it to survive without drawing undue attention to itself.

A VARIABLE KITTEN-CAT

Folds, once mature, will devote a great deal of time to contemplating the world. They will sit very quietly watching everything going on around them. They see no need to be involved in most things. This would burn up energy better reserved for leaping onto your lap for attention, or moving at high speed when they hear the sound of a tin of catfood being opened.

But they do have their moments

The large, well-rounded eyes are separated by a broad nose. Longhair Fold owned by Gary and Diane Finch-Smith.

It is not a breed that will readily take to lead training, for this is not conducive to the way a cat survives through centuries of being a loner. It is intelligent enough to know that this is the best way for a feline to be. After all, it's not a dog—a creature that it will live with but looks down on as being inferior to itself. Its intelligence is thus displayed in a very natural manner.

and will forget their aloof demeanor at times to become the cheeky little kittens they once were. They will grow out of their mischievous period, unlike their foreign cousins, but retain enough youthful charm for them to justifiably be called variable kitten-cats.

This doesn't make them dull; it means they would rather play for short periods with cat toys made for cats rather than invent games, such as climbing up the drapes, knocking ornaments from shelves, or rummaging through drawers that they have learned to open. This sort of behavior just isn't Scottish Fold and is best left to the Asian breeds.

AN INDOOR-OUTDOOR CAT

The Fold is a breed that very much enjoys the outdoors but prefers to reside indoors once the weather changes and becomes wet and cold. The very rugged part of its ancestry is still latent within it, but years of selective breeding have softened the outershell somewhat! Or is it that its intelligence shows through when it has an option?

Like all shorthaired breeds, the Fold needs outdoor time in order to fully exercise its powerful muscles and stimulate its intelligence. It is not that it wishes to climb every tree in sight, or chase anything that moves, but it has a need to feel free to do these things if it wants to. Usually, it will think about them, then have a nap. It enjoys being outside as long as the kitchen door remains open. However, not every Fold is of this disposition. One fact that applies to all felines is that they are very much individuals unto themselves. There are always a few that did not read the book on what they are supposed to be like! But generally, the Fold will be true to its roots for the most part.

It is a breed that will suit just about any sort of home. This is its inheritance, the ability to adjust to any type of environment. It has an obviously unique physical appearance that people will either love or dislike. Its character is far less debatable. If this did not please a potential owner, he will probably not want a cat at all.

Black-and-white Scottish Fold owned by Susan Stephens.

The Fold is a mellow, charming, and thoroughly delightful breed whose quiet and dignified manners are constantly winning it new friends and admirers. It is a cat that delights in being with its owner and can be relied upon to conduct itself in a cheerful, but restrained, manner that makes it so easy to live with. Be warned, once you are owned by a Scottish Fold, it just might spoil you for any other breed: its unique looks hold a thousand ways to charm you.

Something has captured the attention of this Fold kitten.

Red chinchilla tabby and white Longhair Scottish Fold. Owner, Amy and Jean Jones.

DESCRIPTION OF THE BREED

In the world of purebred cats, you will often see or hear references to a standard of the breed. A standard provides a picture—in words—of what is supposed to be the ideal representative of a given breed. It details the breed's physical characteristics and temperament.

Breed standards for cats, drawn up by the various cat associations, may vary from association to association and from country to country. They are subject to change from time to time.

The following standard for the Scottish Fold is that of the Cat Fanciers' Association and is reproduced through the courtesy of that organization.

THE BREED STANDARD

General

The Scottish Fold cat occurred as a spontaneous mutation in farm cats in Scotland. The breed has been established by crosses to British Shorthair and domestic cats in Scotland and England. In America, the outcross is the American and British Shorthair. All bona fide Scottish Fold cats trace their pedigree to Susie, the first fold-ear cat discovered by the founders of the breed, William and Mary Ross.

Head

Well rounded with a firm chin and jaw. Muzzle to have well rounded whisker pads. Head should blend into a short neck. Prominent cheeks with a jowly appearance in males.

Eyes

Wide open with a sweet expression. Large, well rounded, and separated by a broad nose. Eye color to correspond with coat color. Blue-eyed and odd-eyed are allowed for white and white dominated coat patterns, i.e., all van patterns.

Nose

Nose to be short with a gentle curve. A brief stop is permitted, but a definite nose break is considered to be a fault. Profile is moderate in appearance.

Ears

Fold forward and downward. Small, the smaller, tightly folded ear preferred over a loose fold and large ear. The ears should be set in a caplike fashion to expose a rounded cranium. Ear tips to be rounded.

Body

Medium, rounded, and even from shoulder to pelvic girdle. The cat should stand firm on a well padded body. There must be no hint of thickness or lack of mobility in the cat due to short, coarse legs. Toes to be neat and well rounded with five in front and four behind. Overall appearance is that of a

Ears
Fold forward and downward. Small, the smaller, tightly folded ear preferred over a loose fold and large ear.

Head
Well rounded with a firm chin and jaw. Muzzle to have well-rounded whisker pads.

Eyes
Eye color to correspond with coat color.

Nose
Short with a gentle curve.

Body
The cat should stand firm on a well-padded body. There must be no hint of thickness or lack of mobility in the cat due to short, coarse legs.

Tail
The tail should be medium to long but in proportion to the body.

Coat
(Shorthair) Dense, plush, medium short, soft in texture.

well founded cat with medium bone; fault cats obviously lacking in type. Females may be slightly smaller.

Tail

Tail should be medium to long but in proportion to the body. Tail should be flexible and tapering. Longer, tapering tail preferred.

Coat (Shorthair)

Dense, plush, medium-short, soft in texture, full of life. Standing out from body due to density; not flat or close-lying. Coat texture may vary due to color and/or region or seasonal changes.

Coat (Longhair)

Medium to long hair length. Full coat on face and body desirable but short hair permissible on face and legs. Britches, tail plume, toe tufts, and ear furnishings should be clearly visible with a ruff being desirable. *Seriously penalize*: cottony coat, except in kittens.

Disqualify

Kinked tail. Tail that is foreshortened. Tail that is lacking in flexibility due to abnormally thick vertebrae. Splayed toes, incorrect number of toes. Any evidence of illness or poor health.

SCOTTISH FOLD COLORS

White

Pure glistening white. *Nose leather and paw pads*: pink. *Eye color*: deep blue or brilliant gold. Odd-eyed whites shall have one blue and one gold eye with equal color depth.

Black

Dense, coal black, sound from roots to tip of fur. Free from any tinge of rust on tips or smoke undercoat. *Nose leather*: black. *Paw pads*: black or brown. *Eye color*: brilliant gold.

Blue

Blue, lighter shade preferred, one level tone from nose to tip of tail. Sound to roots. A sound darker shade is more acceptable than an unsound lighter shade. *Nose leather and paw pads*: blue. *Eye color*: brilliant gold.

Red

Deep, rich, clear, brilliant red; without shading, markings, or ticking. Lips and chin the same color as coat. *Nose leather and paw pads*: brick red. *Eye color*: brilliant gold.

Cream

One level shade of buff cream, without markings. Sound to the roots. Lighter shades preferred. *Nose leather and paw pads*: pink. *Eye color*: brilliant gold.

Chinchilla Silver

Undercoat pure white. Coat on back, flanks, head and tail sufficiently tipped with black to give the characteristic sparkling silver appearance. Legs may be slightly shaded with tipping. Chin, ear tufts, stomach, and chest, pure white. Rims of eyes, lips, and nose outlined with black. *Nose leather*: brick red. *Paw pads*: black. *Eye color*: green or blue-green.

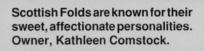

Scottish Folds are known for their sweet, affectionate personalities. Owner, Kathleen Comstock.

Shaded Silver

Undercoat white with a mantle of black tipping shading down from sides, face, and tail from dark on the ridge to white on the chin, chest, stomach, and under the tail. Legs to be the same tone as the face. The general effect to be much darker than a chinchilla. Rims of eyes, lips, and nose outlined with black. *Nose leather*: brick red. *Paw pads*: black. *Eye color*: green or blue-green.

Shaded Cameo (Red Shaded)

Undercoat white with a mantle of red tipping shading down the sides, face, and tail from dark on the ridge to white on the chin, chest, stomach, and under the tail. Legs to be the same tone as face. The general effect to be much redder than the shell cameo. *Nose leather, rims of eyes, and paw pads*: rose. *Eye color*: brilliant gold.

Scottish Folds are companionable cats that enjoy the attention of their human family. Red tabby and white owned by Gayle Rasmussen.

Shell Cameo (Red Chinchilla)

Undercoat white, the coat on the back, flanks, head, and tail to be sufficiently tipped with red to give the characteristic sparkling appearance. Face and legs may be very slightly shaded with tipping. Chin, ear tufts, stomach, and chest white. *Nose leather and paw pads*: rose. *Eye color*: brilliant gold.

Black Smoke

White undercoat, deeply tipped with black. Cat in repose appears black. In motion, the white undercoat is clearly apparent. Points and mask black with narrow band of white at base of hairs next to skin which may be seen only when fur is parted. *Nose leather and paw pads*: black. *Eye color*: brilliant gold.

A playful silver mackerel tabby. In addition to this tabby pattern, Folds also come in patched and classic tabby patterns. Owner, Sandy Greenbaum.

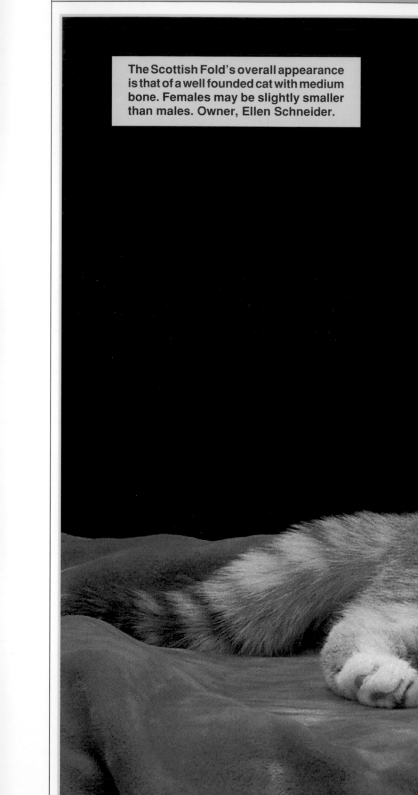

The Scottish Fold's overall appearance is that of a well founded cat with medium bone. Females may be slightly smaller than males. Owner, Ellen Schneider.

Blue Smoke

White undercoat, deeply tipped with blue. Cat in repose appears blue. In motion, the white undercoat is clearly apparent. Points and mask blue with narrow band of white at base of hairs which may be seen only when the fur is parted. *Nose leather and paw pads*: blue. *Eye color*: Brilliant gold.

Classic Tabby Pattern

Markings dense, clearly defined, and broad. Legs evenly barred with bracelets coming up to meet the body markings. Tail evenly ringed. Several unbroken necklaces on neck and upper chest, the more the better. Frown marks on forehead form an intricate letter "M." Unbroken line runs back from outer corner of

The Scottish Fold's coat should stand out from the body due to density. It should not be flat or close-lying. Owner, Kathleen Comstock.

Cameo Smoke (Red Smoke)

White undercoat, deeply tipped with red. Cat in repose appears red. In motion, the white undercoat is clearly apparent. Points and mask red with narrow band of white at base of hairs next to skin which may be seen only when fur is parted. *Nose leather, rims of eyes, and paw pads*: rose. *Eye color*: brilliant gold.

eye. Swirls on cheeks. Vertical lines over back of head extend to shoulder markings, which are in the shape of a butterfly with both upper and lower wings distinctly outlined and marked with dots inside outline. Back markings consist of a vertical line down the spine from butterfly to tail with a vertical stripe paralleling it on each side, the three stripes well separated by stripes of the ground

In Longhair Scottish Folds, the coat is medium to long in length. A full coat on the face and body is desirable, but short hair is permissible on the face and legs. Red chinchilla tabby and white owned by Amy and Jean Jones.

color. Large solid blotch on each side to be encircled by one or more unbroken rings. Side markings should be the same on both sides. Double vertical rows of buttons on chest and stomach.

Mackerel Tabby Pattern

Markings dense, clearly defined, and all narrow pencillings. Legs evenly barred with narrow bracelets coming up to meet the body markings. Tail barred. Necklaces on neck and chest distinct, like so many chains. Head barred with an "M" on the forehead. Unbroken lines running back from the eyes. Lines running down the head to the shoulders. Spine lines run together to form a narrow saddle. Narrow pencillings run around body.

Patched Tabby Pattern

A patched tabby (torbie) is an established silver, brown, or blue tabby with patches of red and/or cream.

Spotted Tabby Pattern

Markings on the body to be spotted. The spots can be round, oblong, or rosette shaped. Any of these are of equal merit, but the spots, however shaped or placed, shall be distinct. Spots should not run together in a broken Mackerel pattern. A dorsal stripe runs the length of the body to the tip of the tail. The stripe is ideally composed of spots. The markings on the face and forehead shall be typically tabby markings. Underside of the body to have "vest buttons." Legs and tail are barred.

Britches, tail plume, toe tufts, and ear furnishings should be clearly visible, with a ruff being desirable.

Black-and-white bi-color Fold. Owner, Linda Swierczynski.

Silver Tabby

Ground color, including lips and chin, pale clear silver. Markings dense black. *Nose leather*: brick red. *Paw pads*: black. *Eye color*: green or hazel.

Blue Silver Tabby (Pewter Tabby)

Ground color, including lips and chin, pale, clear, bluish silver. Markings sound blue. *Nose leather*: blue or old rose trimmed with blue. *Paw pads*: blue.

Blue Silver (Pewter)

Undercoat white with a mantle of blue tipping shading down from sides, face, and tail from dark on the ridge to white on the chin, chest, underside and under the tail. Legs to be the same tone as the face. *Rims of eyes, lips and*

nose: outlined with blue. *Nose leather*: blue or old rose trimmed with blue. *Paw pads*: blue.

Red Tabby

Ground color red. Markings deep, rich red. Lips and chin red. *Nose leather and paw pads*: brick red. *Eye color*: brilliant gold.

Brown Tabby

Ground color brilliant coppery brown. Markings dense black. Lips and chin the same shade as the rings around the eyes. Back of leg black from paw to heel. *Nose leather*: brick red. *Paw pads*: black or brown. *Eye color*: brilliant gold.

Blue Tabby

Ground color, including lips

and chin, pale bluish ivory. Markings a very deep blue affording a good contrast with ground color. Warm fawn overtones or patina over the whole. *Nose leather*: old rose. *Paw Pads*: rose. *Eye color*: brilliant gold.

Cream Tabby

Ground color, including lips and chin, very pale cream. Marking of buff or cream sufficiently darker than the ground color to afford good contrast but remaining within the dilute color range. *Nose leather and paw pads*: pink. *Eye color*: brilliant gold.

Cameo Tabby

Ground color off-white. Markings red. *Nose leather and paw pads*: rose. *Eye color*: brilliant gold.

Tortoiseshell

Black with unbrindled patches of red and cream. Patches clearly defined and well broken on both body and extremities. Blaze of red or cream on face is desirable. *Eye color*: brilliant copper.

Calico

White with unbrindled patches of black and red. White predominant on underparts. *Eye color*: brilliant gold.

Dilute Calico

White with unbrindled patches of blue and cream. White predominant on underparts. *Eye color*: brilliant gold.

Blue-Cream

Blue with patches of solid cream. Patches clearly defined and well broken on both body and extremities. *Eye color*: brilliant gold.

Head study of a red tabby and white Scottish Fold. Owner, Gayle Rasmussen.

Bi-color

White with unbrindled patches of black, white with unbrindled patches of blue, white with unbrindled patches of red, or white with unbrindled patches of cream. *Eye color*: brilliant gold.

OSFC (Other Scottish Fold Colors)

Any other color or pattern with the exception of those showing evidence of hybridization resulting in the colors chocolate, lavender, the Himalayan pattern, or these combinations with white. *Eye color*: appropriate to the dominant color of the cat.

***Scottish Fold allowable outcross breeds*: British Shorthair, American Shorthair.**

Silver classic tabby and white Longhair Scottish Fold. Owner, Gary and Diane Finch Smith.

SELECTING A SCOTTISH FOLD

THE QUALITY OF YOUR PET

Scottish Folds come in a range of qualities from the inferior, through the typical examples of the breed, to those which are show winners, or at least potentially so. You may wish to own a high-quality Scottish Fold even though you have no intention to show it. Quality means it will have good bone conformation, the correct stature, and its color or patterns will be of a high standard. Such a cat will be a costly purchase. A typical Scottish Fold will be just that. It will display no glaring faults and its color will be sound. It may display some minor failings in type or color that would preclude it from ever being of show quality.

An inferior Scottish Fold will be one which has obvious faults, either its conformation, its coat quality, poor color or in other ways inferior. Such cats are often described as being pet quality. As long as you appreciate that this term means inferior, its use is fine. However, there are two kinds of inferior Scottish Folds. There is the cat which is inferior only in respect to its type and color—not in relation to its basic structure and health.

There is then the inferior cat produced by those who are in Scottish Folds just to make money. These people have cats that they breed with no consideration for the vigor of the offspring. Such kittens are invariably sickly and prone to illnesses throughout their lives. Poor health and inferior Scottish Folds result from unplanned matings and excessive breeding, coupled with a lack of ongoing selection being applied to future breeding stock.

How do you make the right choice when selecting a Scottish Fold? The answer is you do your homework. Visit shows, talk to established exhibitors, and judges. When you visit the seller take a good look at his stock, and more especially the living conditions of the cats. Is he giving you the hard sell, or does he seem more concerned about the kitten's future home? Sometimes the dedicated seller might even annoy you, but he is concerned for his kittens, even if they are not quality Scottish Folds. The more Scottish Folds you see, the more likely you are to make a wise choice.

WHICH SEX TO PURCHASE?

From the viewpoint of pet suitability, there really is no difference between a tom (male) and a queen (female). Some people prefer one sex, but this is purely subjective. This author has found males to be more consistent in their character than females, who may tend to be "all or nothing" in their attitude. In other words, they can be extremely

A good specimen of the breed will have good bone conformation, the correct stature, and coat color/pattern that is of a high standard. Tri-color owned by Michael E. Nelson.

affectionate one day, but rather standoffish the next. The tom tends to be much the same from one day to the next, whatever his character might be.

It really is a pot-luck matter just how affectionate a kitten will grow up to become. Cats are very much individuals, and they can change as they grow up. The way they are treated also affects their personality. Therefore, it is more a case of selecting a kitten that appeals to you, regardless of its sex.

Of course, if you wish to become a breeder then the female has to be the better choice. Once she reaches breeding age you can then select a suitable mate for her from the hundreds of quality stud males available to you. If you purchase a male with the view to owning a stud, you are really gambling that he will mature into a fine cat that others would want to use. For this to happen, your tom would need to be very successful in the show ring, and then in the quality of his offspring.

Furthermore, owning a whole tom (a male that has not been neutered) does present more practical problems than owning a queen. Such a male will be continually marking his territory (your furniture) by spraying it with his urine, which is hardly a fragrant scent!

If your Scottish Fold is to be a pet only, then regardless of the sex you should have it neutered or spayed. It will be more affectionate to you, will not be wandering off looking for romance, and will not shed its coat as excessively as would an unaltered Scottish Fold. In the case of a tom, he will not come home with pieces of his ears missing as a result of his fights with other entire males. Your queen will not present you with kittens that you do not want but which she will have if she is not spayed. She is far less likely to spray than is the male, but she will show her desire to mate, both with her "calling" sounds, which can be eerie, and her provocative crouching position in which she is clearly inviting a mating.

WHAT AGE TO PURCHASE?

Breeders vary in the age they judge a kitten ready for a new home. An important consideration is obviously if the new owners have experience of cats generally and kittens in particular. While an eight-week-old baby is quite delightful, it is invariably better from a health standpoint that the kitten remains with its mother until it is ten or more weeks of age. Some breeders will not part with a kitten until it is 16 weeks of age.

The kitten should have received at least temporary vaccinations against feline distemper and rabies (if applicable in your country and if the kitten is over 12 weeks of age) and preferably protection against other major feline infections. Additionally, you should let your own vet examine your Scottish Fold.

Although most owners will wish to obtain a kitten, a potential breeder or exhibitor may find that

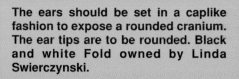

The ears should be set in a caplike fashion to expose a rounded cranium. The ear tips are to be rounded. Black and white Fold owned by Linda Swierczynski.

The Longhair Scottish Fold will require more grooming than its shorthaired counterpart. Red and white van Fold owned by Gary and Diane Finch-Smith.

a young adult (over eight to nine months of age) is more suitable to his needs. By this age the quality of the Scottish Fold is becoming more apparent. However, bear in mind that a mature Scottish Fold queen will not be at her peak until she is about two years of age. A tom will be even later in reaching full maturity, and he may not peak until he is five years of age.

ONE OR TWO SCOTTISH FOLDS?

Without any doubt, two kittens are always preferred to one. They provide constant company for each other and are a delight to watch as they play. The extra costs involved in their upkeep are unlikely to be a factor if you are able to afford a Scottish Fold in the first place.

Black smoke and white Scottish Fold. Owner, Gwen Hornung.

GENERAL CARE & GROOMING

Scottish Fold cats are extremely easy to cater to in terms of their accommodations and general care. This chapter will discuss purchasing the essential and nonessential accessories for your cat, socializing your cat with children and other animals, making a safe environment for your cat, and disciplining your cat the proper and most effective way.

ABSOLUTE ESSENTIALS

While keeping a cat is essentially a simple task, there are certain items that the cat owner absolutely must have if he expects to keep his kitty happy and well. The following items should be purchased from your local pet store or supply center before you bring the cat into your home. Don't try to find bargains! Buy the best the first time and you won't have to replace it as often. Pet shops offer the finest pet supplies, and the proprietors will be happy to advise you which is the most effective and best for your particular cat.

Litter Tray

Every cat will need a litter tray so that it can relieve itself whenever it wishes to. If this is not provided from the outset, the only possible consequence is that the cat will be forced to foul your carpet or some other surface. There are many styles and sizes of litter trays, and the larger ones are the best for long-term service. Some have igloo-type hoods, both to provide a sense of privacy for the cat and to retain any odors. However, an open tray is just as good and will not in any case be foul smelling if it is cleaned as it should be.

You will need to purchase cat litter for the base of the tray. There are many brands to choose from, and some have odor neutralizers already in them. Cover the base with enough litter to absorb urine and for the cat to scratch around in. In the event you should run out of litter, you can use coarse grade sawdust or wood shavings. These are preferred to garden soil because the latter may contain the eggs of parasitic worms or other parasites.

The tray should be cleaned after each use, removing that which is soiled. A small dustpan is handy for attending to this chore. Once a week, you should disinfect and thoroughly rinse the tray.

Housetraining is easily accomplished with a kitten. When you see it searching for somewhere to relieve itself, which will be accompanied by crying, it should be gently lifted and placed into its tray. Never scold a kitten for fouling the floor: it will not understand why you are annoyed with it. You must watch the kitten after it has played and after it wakes up because these are prime times for it to want to relieve itself. Remember, kittens cannot control their bowel movements for more than a few seconds; this time increases considerably as the cat matures. If you exhibit patience, you will find the kitty quickly gets to know what is expected of it. Cats are fastidious about cleanliness, so if they foul the home, there is invariably a reason for so doing. Often it will be because the litter tray has not been cleaned or you were not around enough when the cat was a kitten.

Scratching Post

Here again, there are many styles to choose from. All have a fabric on them, and the post may be free standing or the sort that is screwed to a wall. You can also purchase carpet-clad climbing frames, which are more expensive but greatly enjoyed by cats. When you see your kitten or cat go to scratch your armchair, lift it up and place it against the scratching post. Gently draw its front feet down the post a few times. Again, if this is repeated a number of times, the kitten will understand that it can claw away on the post but not on the furniture. As it grows older, it will no doubt test your resolve now and then, but usually if you clap your hands and say "No" in a firm voice, it will realize you are keeping an eye on it!

Cat Collar

All cats should wear a cat collar fitted with an ID tag. In many cities, this is a law. An elastic collar will prevent the possibility of its getting snagged, thus possibly choking the cat. Be sure it is neither too tight nor too loose. You should be able to place a finger between the collar and the cat's neck.

Carry Box

The carry box is so useful that I regard it as an essential item for all cat owners. It will be needed when you visit the vet, when traveling, or when you need to contain the cat for any reason. It also makes a fine bed for a kitten. The box can be made of wicker, wood, wire, or fiberglass. The latter are probably the best but can be expensive if they are of a high quality. It is essential that they should be large enough for the adult cat to stand upright in and not be forced to stoop.

The base of the box can be fitted with a good lining of newspaper on which a blanket is placed. A kitten will find this a nice bed, especially if it has a companion. If not, place a cuddly toy in with it to snuggle up against. When it is a kitten and during its first week or so in its new home, it is better that it is confined at night, so it cannot harm itself by wandering about the home. Once it is totally familiar with your home, you can leave the carry-box door open at night so it can come and go as it wishes.

Feeding Dishes

You will want one dish for moist cat food, one for dry food, and one for water. You can purchase dishes made of earthenware, aluminum, stainless steel, or plastic. You can

A cat carrier for your Fold is a must. It is the ideal way to transport your pet to the vet, on vacation, and the like. Owner, Amy and Jean Jones.

Finishing touches when grooming a Longhair Scottish Fold. After brushing, comb the coat with a medium-toothed comb to remove any loose hair. Folds with long hair should be groomed at least twice weekly to keep their coats in top condition.

also use saucers or any combination of these. The main thing is that they are kept spotlessly clean, so they should be washed after each use. The water dish should be cleaned and replenished each day.

Brush

Cats do not come any simpler to groom than a Scottish Fold. Even so, your cat should have its own brush, preferably of a medium-bristle type. A chamois leather or silk cloth is also useful to give your cat that extra sheen after it has been brushed. Although the Scottish Fold hardly needs any brushing, it is useful to attend to this once a week. This makes your cat familiar with being handled, and at such a time, you can give it a check over. Inspect its ears to see that they are free of wax and check the teeth to see that they are clean. Inspect the pads to ensure that they are firm but supple. Part the toes with your fingers just to make sure they are free of debris. Lodged in the skin, dirt and grass could be the source of an abscess if they are not removed. Gently feel the abdomen to check that there are no swellings.

Requiring more grooming than the shorthaired variety, the Longhair Scottish Fold will need both a brush and a comb. Begin by gently brushing the coat in the direction of its lie to remove loose hair and dirt. Then brush again, this time against the lie of the hair. To finish, comb the coat with a medium-toothed comb. It is best to brush the longhaired cat no fewer than twice per week in order to keep the coat healthy and free of mats and tangles.

BEYOND THE BASICS

Pet lovers love to lavish their pets with all kinds of goodies, and for a cat owner, the sky is the limit when it comes to choosing special accessories for his pet. The ever-expanding pet industry makes it easy for cat owners to find new and inventive ways to entertain and better care for their feline friends.

Basket or Bed

If you obtain a carry box for your kitten, then a bed is not a necessity. Cats like to choose their own place to sleep, and indeed they will have numerous places depending on their mood, the ambient temperature, and who happens to be in your home at a given time. Some will have a favorite chair or sofa, some may prefer a secluded spot behind a chair, while others will prefer to sleep on your bed, knowing this to be a warm and popular place with their "human-cat" companions.

Better than a conventional basket would be to invest in one of the many carpet-clad, wooden furniture pieces produced these days for cats. These are fun and take into account the cat's preference for sleeping above floor level. Some cats do sleep in baskets, so it is a case of reviewing all the options and deciding which you think will best meet your needs.

Halter or Harness

If you plan on taking your cat with you on vacation or generally when you travel, it will be found that a cat collar does not offer you full control over your Scottish Fold. Additionally to the collar, you could purchase one of the numerous halters now available for cats. Choose one that fits snugly. Those with top fastenings are easy to place on your cat. Do not obtain dog harnesses because they will be too big around the chest, even if they are for small dogs.

Lead training is best done while your pet is young. Place the halter on the kitten and let it become familiar with it before you attempt to attach the lead. When the halter does not bother the cat, you can then attach the lead and let the cat wander about in the privacy of your yard. Here it will become used to the fact that there is a restraint on its movements. The process cannot be hurried because cats do not like to be restricted. Only devote a few minutes per day to lead training and always encourage the cat with a treat.

Do not take the cat from the confines of its home territory until it is really relaxed on a lead. In the event of a dog suddenly appearing, the halter allows you to maintain control of the cat, which should be promptly lifted

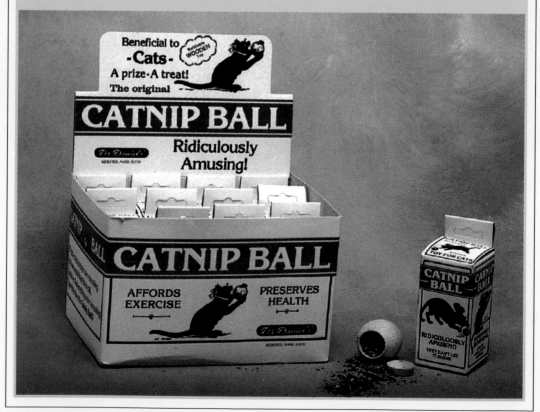

Catnip has long been a feline favorite. It is available in many forms and is a popular cat treat. Photo courtesy of Dr. A.C. Daniels.

Good grooming habits should start at an early age. Your pet shop can help you select the proper grooming aids for your cat. Photo courtesy of The Kong Company.

up. If it is not your intention to take your cat on regular outings, there is little point in lead training it because cats are generally not happy away from their home range.

Toys

There is no shortage of commercially made cat toys these days. Avoid soft, plastic ones that your pet might break apart and swallow pieces from. If you devote time to playing with your cats, you will find that they will learn how to play games with you, and it will strengthen the bond between you and your cat.

CATS AND CHILDREN

If there are young children in your home, it is most important that they are taught from the outset to respect your new kitten or cat. Children must understand that cats should not be disturbed if they are sleeping and should not be handled in an incorrect manner. When being lifted, a cat should never be grasped by the loose fur on its neck. Always support the full body weight with one hand, while securing the cat firmly but gently around the neck with the other hand.

Children should be made aware of the fact that even kittens can inflict a nasty scratch on them if the kitten is not treated with kindness and consideration. Essentially, you must always be watchful if young children are playing with the family cat until they are old enough to understand how it must be handled.

CATS AND OTHER PETS

The cat is a prime predator and should not be left in the company of young rabbits, guinea pigs, hamsters, or mice if these other pets are out of their cage. As a general rule, if a pet is as big as your cat or is another carnivore, it will usually be safe. Cats and dogs get on really well if they are brought up together. However, if a kitten is introduced into a home that has an adult dog, due care must be exercised. The first thing to ensure is that the resident pet gets extra attention so it does not become jealous of the new arrival.

The kitten and other pets must come to terms with each other in their own time and manner — it is not something you can hurry. In some instances, a newly acquired cat may make friends very quickly with dogs or other household cats. In other cases, the best that ever happens is a sort of truce, each accepting the other but avoiding contact most of the time. Kittens will invariably be accepted much more readily than will adult cats. The latter, of course, will have developed their own attitudes to other animals depending on what their experiences have been with them.

SAFEGUARDING A KITTEN

When a kitten is first introduced to your home, there are many potential dangers that it must be protected from. For example, a door left ajar on a windy day could easily slam shut on the kitty. An unprotected balcony is an obvious danger to a young feline, as is a garden pond. An open fire is yet another example of how a kitten might easily become injured. They are, of course, naturally cautious of dangerous situations, but even so, it is best to watch out for them just as their mother would.

The kitchen is probably the most dangerous place for kittens. A typical scenario is that you might turn around from the stove with a pan of boiling water or a kettle in your hand, only to trip over the kitten. The water may scald the kitten or yourself badly, and the fall would not do you any good either! Kittens just love to pounce and hang onto string and its like. The latter might be the cord from an electric iron you are using -— the result being obvious. As your Scottish Fold gets a little older, it will easily be able to jump onto kitchen units and should be educated at an early age not to do this in this particular room.

The other important area of safeguarding a kitten is in relation to ensuring it is given maximum protection against major feline diseases. This is done via vaccinations. Consult your vet about these as soon as you have obtained your Scottish Fold. Do not allow the kitten out of the house until it has complete protection.

DISCIPLINE

Cats are very intelligent and respond to discipline just as dogs and most other comparable pets will. They are not dangerous to

The Scottish Fold's head should blend into a short neck. Cheeks are prominent, with well-developed jowls in males. Black smoke and white owned by Gwen Hornung.

Like other breeds of cat, Folds like to play with objects that they can easily manipulate with their paws.

people so do not need the level of training that a dog does to fit into a human world. It's really a case in which your cat should understand one simple command—"no." If it goes to scratch the furniture, you should promptly lift it up and say, "No." A very light tap on its rump will enforce the command. This is about the extent of discipline that will ever be needed.

You should never need to use discipline with a cat. If you think carefully about any given action and apply an appropriate response fairly and consistently (the latter being crucial), you will develop a real understanding with your feline friend.

Brown tabby Longhair Scottish Fold. Owner, JoAnn Hinkle.

FEEDING YOUR SCOTTISH FOLD

Cats and kittens are very much like people when it comes to their eating habits. Some are extremely easy to satisfy; others are much more difficult to please. Adult cats can be a worry, but at least you know they must have eaten something to have survived to maturity. Kittens, on the other hand, can prematurely turn your hair gray because you fear they may not thrive unless you can come up with some delicacy that tempts their palate!

Fortunately, there are so many quality brands of commercial cat foods available today that it should be possible to get even the most fastidious of kittens through its most difficult early months.

CATS ARE CARNIVORES

The cat is a prime predator in its wild habitat, and this means its basic diet must be composed of the flesh of other animals, be they mammals, birds, or fish. The digestive tract of a carnivore has evolved to cope with proteins, but it has little ability to digest raw vegetable matter. This means the latter must first be boiled, so that the hard cellulose walls of such foods are softened, then broken down by the digestive juices and flora found in the alimentary tract.

In the wild, the cat would eat just about every part of its prey,
leaving only the bones that were too large for it to digest. This diet would provide proteins and fats from the body tissues, roughage from the fur or feathers, and carbohydrates and vitamins from the partially digested vegetable matter that would be in the intestines of the prey. Combined with water, a very well-balanced diet would be provided for the cat. An equivalent of such nutrition is what you must strive to supply.

COMMERCIAL FOODS

The range of commercial cat foods encompasses canned, semi-moist, and dry diets. We have always found that our cats have never really enjoyed any of the semi-moist foods. The canned and dry foods come in an extensive range of flavors, which include meat, fish, and poultry. Of the canned foods, some have a firm consistency; others are chunks in a sauce. There are also formulated kitten foods.

Commercial foods can form the basis of your Scottish Fold's diet, but you should supply a variety of them to reduce the chances that some key constituent is missing from the diet. Scottish Folds will no doubt help in this matter because they seem to tire of one brand if it is fed daily. Indeed, deciding which is their chosen flavor of the week can be an interesting guessing game. They will suddenly show no interest in a product they seemed to eat with relish just a few days earlier! You will find that some cats enjoy fish flavors, others poultry and yet others, the various meats.

Dry food is enjoyed by most, though not all, Scottish Folds. It provides good exercise for the teeth and jaw muscles, which canned foods do not. Their other advantage is that you can leave them out all day without their losing their appeal to your pets, or attracting flies. Water must always be available to your cats; this is even more important if the basic diet is of dried foods.

Treats can be provided on an occasional basis to help provide a little variety in the diet. Some treats act as a cleansing agent to help reduce tartar on the cat's teeth. Photo courtesy of Heinz.

are appreciated, but only give small quantities of them as a treat because they may prove too rich for your pet's system. Chicken is enjoyed by nearly all cats.

Cheese, egg yolk, spaghetti, and even boiled rice are all items that you can offer to your pets to see if it appeals to them. Small beef and other meat bones that still have some meat on them will be enjoyed and keep a kitten or cat amused for quite some time. Beware of bones that easily splinter, such as those of chicken or rabbit.

You can by all means see if small pieces of vegetables or fruits are accepted if mixed with the food, but generally cats will leave them. This is no problem providing that the cat is receiving commercial foods as its basic diet. Such products are all fortified with essential vitamins after the cooking process.

NON-COMMERCIAL FOODS

Your Scottish Fold will enjoy many of the foods that you eat. These foods provide both variety and good exercise for the jaws. Human consumption meats can be of beef, pork, or lamb. All fish should be steamed or boiled, and it is best to stay with white fish such as cod. Tuna, sardines, and other canned fish

HOW MUCH TO FEED?

Cats prefer to eat a little but often, rather than consume one mighty meal a day. However, as carnivores, adults are well able to cope with one large meal a day. The same is not true of kittens, which should receive three or four meals per day. A kitten or a cat will normally only consume that which is needed. You can arrive at this amount by trial and error. If kitty devours its meal and is looking for more, then let it have more. You will quickly be able to judge how much each kitten needs to satisfy itself. Always remove any moist foods that are uneaten after each meal.

At 12 weeks of age the kitten should have four meals a day. One of these meals can be omitted when the kitten is 16 weeks old, but increase the quantity of the other three. You can reduce to two meals a day when the kitten is about nine months of age. From that age, it is best to continue feeding two meals—one in the morning and one in the early evening. How many times a day you feed your adult cat is unimportant. The key factor is that it receives as much as it needs over the day, and that the diet is balanced to provide the essential ingredients discussed earlier. It is also better that meals are given regularly. Cats, like humans, are creatures of habit.

WATER

If a cat's diet is essentially of moist foods, it will drink far less than if the diet is basically of dry foods. Many cats do not like faucet (tap) water because they are able to smell and taste the many additives included by your local water board. Chlorine is high on this list. Although it dissipates into the air quite readily, chloromides do not, which is why the cat may ignore the water. During the filtering process at the water station, chemicals are both taken out and added. The resulting mineral balance and taste are often not to a cat's liking. This is why you will see cats drinking from puddles, a flower vase, or even your toilet, because the taste is better for them. If your water is refused, then you can see if your cat prefers mineralized bottled water—not distilled because the latter has no mineral content to it.

THE NEW ARRIVAL

It is a very traumatic time for a kitten when it leaves its mother and siblings. It will often eat well the first day; however, as it starts to miss its family, it will fret. You can reduce its stress by providing the diet it was receiving from the seller. You can change the diet slowly, if necessary, as it settles down. Of course, many kittens have no problems, but if yours does, this feeding advice should help its period of adjustment.

What is essential is that the kitten takes in sufficient liquids so that it does not start to dehydrate. This, more than anything else, will adversely affect its health very rapidly. If you are at all concerned, do consult your vet. The kitten may have picked up a virus, but if it is treated promptly, this should not be a problem. Your vet might supply you with a dietary supplement, which we have found excellent for kittens experiencing "new home syndrome."

KEEPING YOUR SCOTTISH FOLD HEALTHY

Like any other animal, your Scottish Fold can fall victim to hundreds of diseases and conditions. Most can be prevented by sound husbandry. The majority, should they be recognized in their early stages, can be treated with modern drugs or by surgery. Clearly, preventive techniques are better and less costly than treatments, yet in many instances a cat will become ill because the owner has neglected some basic aspect of general management. In this chapter, we are not so much concerned with cataloging all the diseases your cat could contract, because these are legion, but more concerned with reviewing sound management methods.

A scratching post and toys are necessities for any cat-owning household. The post will help deter your pet's scratching furniture and draperies, and toys will amuse him for hours on end.

HYGIENE

Always apply routine hygiene to all aspects of your pet's management. This alone dramatically reduces the chances of your pet becoming ill because it restricts pathogens (disease-causing organisms) from building up colonies that are able to overcome the natural defense mechanisms of your Scottish Fold.

1. After your cat has eaten its fill of any moist foods, either discard the food or keep it for later by placing it in your refrigerator. Anything left uneaten at the end of the day can be trashed. Always wash the bowl after each meal. Do not feed your pet from any dishes that are chipped, cracked, or, in the case of plastic, those that are badly scratched.

2. Always store food in a dry, cool cupboard or in the refrigerator in the case of fresh foods.

3. For whatever reason, if you have been handling someone else's cats, always wash your hands before handling your own cats.

4. Be rigorous in cleaning your cat's litter box as soon as you see that it has been fouled.

5. Pay particular attention to the grooming of a Scottish Fold cat because so many problems can begin with a seemingly innocuous event. For example, in itself, a minor cut may not be a major problem as long as it is treated with an antiseptic. But if it is left as an open untreated wound, it is an obvious site for bacterial colonization. The bacteria then gain access to the bloodstream, and a major problem ensues that might not even be associated with the initial wound. The same applies to flea or lice bites. Inspect the skin carefully for signs of flea droppings when you groom a Scottish Fold. These appear like minute specks of black dust.

RECOGNIZING AN ILL CAT

You must be able to recognize when your cat is ill in order to seek a solution to the problem. You must learn to distinguish between a purely temporary condition and that which will need some form of veterinary advice and/or treatment. For example, a cat can sprain a muscle by jumping and landing awkwardly. This would normally correct itself over a 36-48 hour period. Your pet may contract a slight chill, or its feces might become loose. Both conditions will normally correct themselves over a day or so. On the other hand, if a condition persists for more than two days, it would be advisable to telephone your vet for advice.

In general, any appearance or behavior that is not normal for your cat would suggest something is responsible for the abnormality. This is your first indication that something may be amiss. The following are a number of signs that indicate a problem:

1. Diarrhea, especially if it is very liquid, foul-smelling or blood-streaked. If blood is seen in the urine, this is also an indication of a problem, as is excessive straining or cries of pain when the cat tries to relieve itself.

2. Discharge from the nose or eyes. Many Scottish Folds may discharge a liquid from the eyes due to blocked tear ducts. This is associated with the foreshortening of the muzzle. However, an excessive discharge needs veterinary attention.

3. Repeated vomiting. All cats are sick occasionally with indigestion. They will also vomit after eating grass, but repeated vomiting is not normal.

4. Wheezing sounds when breathing, or any other suggestion of breathing difficulties.

5. Excessive scratching. All cats will have a good scratch on a quite regular basis, but excessive scratching indicates a skin problem, especially if it has created sores or lesions.

6. Constant rubbing of the rear end along the ground.

7. Bald patches, lesions, cuts, and swellings on the body, legs, tail, or face.

8. The coat seems to lack bounce or life, and is dull.

9. The cat is listless and lethargic, showing little interest in what is going on around it.

10. The eyes have a glazed look to them, or the haw (nictitating

membrane, or third eyelid) is clearly visible.

11. The cat is displaying an unusual lack of interest in its favorite food items.

12. The gums of the teeth seem very red or swollen.

13. Fits or other abnormal signs of behavior.

14. Any obvious pain or distress.

Very often two or more clinical signs will be apparent when a condition is developing. The number of signs increases as the disease or ailment advances to a more sinister stage.

DIAGNOSIS

Correct diagnosis is of the utmost importance before any form of treatment can be administered. Often it will require blood and/or fecal microscopy in order to establish the exact cause of a condition. Many of the signs listed above are common to most diseases, so never attempt home diagnosis and treatment: if you are wrong, your cherished Scottish Fold may pay for your error with its life. Once ill health is suspected, any lost time favors the pathogens and makes treatment both more difficult and more costly.

In making your original decision to purchase a Scottish Fold, or any other cat, you should always have allowed for the cost of veterinary treatment. If this is likely to be a burden that you cannot afford, then do not purchase a cat. The first few months, and especially the first weeks, is the time when most cats will become ill. If they survive this period, the chances are that future visits to the vet will be rare, other than for booster vaccinations.

Kittens do not have the immunity to pathogens that the adult cat does, nor do they have the muscle reserves of the adult. If they are ill, they need veterinary help very quickly if they are to have a good chance of overcoming a disease or major problem.

Having decided that your cat is not well, you should make notes on paper of the signs of the problem, when you first noticed them, and how quickly things have deteriorated. If possible, obtain a fecal and urine sample, then telephone your vet and make an appointment. Ask other cat owners in your area who their vet is. Some vets display a greater liking for cats, or dogs, or horses than do others. This is just human nature, but obviously you want to go to one that has a special affection for felines.

TREATMENT

Once your vet has prescribed a course of treatment, it is important that you follow it exactly as instructed. Do not discontinue the medicine because the cat shows a big improvement. Such an action could prove counterproductive, and the pathogens that had not been killed might develop an immunity to the treatment. A relapse could occur, and this might be more difficult to deal with.

VACCINATIONS

There are a few extremely dangerous diseases that afflict cats, but fortunately there are vaccines that can dramatically reduce the risk of them infecting your Scottish Fold. The bacteria and viruses that cause such diseases are often found in the air wherever there are cats. Discuss a program of immunization with your vet.

When a kitten is born, it inherits protection from disease via the colostrum of its mother's milk. Such protection may last for up to 16 weeks—but it varies from kitten to kitten and may last only six weeks. It is therefore recommended that your kitten be vaccinated against diseases at six to eight weeks of age just to be on the safe side. Boosters are required some weeks later and thereafter each year. Potential breeding females should be given boosters about three to four weeks prior to the due date. This will ensure that a high level of antibodies is passed to the kittens.

An important consideration with regard to the major killer

A healthy Scottish Fold will have bright, clear eyes and a dry nose.

diseases in cats is the treatment of infection. If a cat survives an infection, it will probably be a carrier of the disease and shed the pathogens continually throughout its life. The only safe course is therefore to ensure that your kittens are protected. The main diseases for which there are vaccinations are as follows:

Rabies: This is a disease of the neurological system. It is non-existent in Great Britain, Ireland, Australia, New Zealand, Hawaii, certain oceanic islands, Holland, Sweden, and Norway. In these countries, extremely rigid quarantine laws are applied to ensure it stays that way. You cannot have your cat vaccinated against rabies if you live in one of these countries, unless you are about to emigrate with your cat. In all other countries, rabies vaccinations are either compulsory or strongly advised. They are given when the kitten is three or more months of age.

Feline panleukopenia: Also known as feline infectious enteritis, and feline distemper.

This is a highly contagious viral disease. Vaccinations are given when the kitten is about eight weeks old, and a booster is given four weeks later. In high-risk areas, a third injection may be advised four weeks after the second one.

Feline respiratory disease complex: Often referred to as cat flu but this is incorrect. Although a number of diseases are within this group, two of them are especially dangerous. They are feline viral rhinotracheitis (FVR) and feline calicivirus (FCV). The vaccination for the prevention of these diseases is combined and given when the kitten is six or more weeks of age; a booster follows three to four weeks later.

Feline leukemia virus complex (FeLV): This disease was first recognized in 1964, and a vaccine became available in the US in about 1985. Like "cat flu," the name is misleading, because it is far more complex than a blood cancer, which is what its name implies. Essentially, it destroys the cat's immune system, so the cat may contract any of the major diseases.

The disease is easily spread via the saliva of a cat as it licks other cats. It is also spread prenatally from an infected queen to her offspring via the blood, or when washing her kittens. This is why it is important to test all breeding cats for FeLV. Vaccination is worthwhile only on a kitten or cat that has tested negative. If a cat tests positive for the disease, it has a 70 percent chance of survival, though it will be a carrier in many instances.

Feline infectious peritonitis (FIP): This disease has various effects on the body's metabolism. There are no satisfactory tests for it, but intranasal liquid vaccinations via a dropper greatly reduce the potential for it to develop in the tissues of the nose.

PARASITES

Parasites are organisms that live on or in a host. They feed from it without providing any benefit in return. External parasites include fleas, lice, ticks, flies, and any other creature that bites the skin of the cat. Internal parasites include all pathogens, but the term is more commonly applied to worms in their various forms.

External parasites and their eggs can be seen with the naked eye. All can be eradicated with treatment from your vet. However, initial treatment will need to be followed by further treatments because most compounds are ineffective on the eggs. The repeat treatments kill the larvae as they hatch. It is also important that all bedding be treated or destroyed because this is often where parasites prefer to live when not on the host.

All cats are host to a range of worm species. If worms multiply in the cat, they adversely affect its health. They will cause loss of appetite, wasting, and a steady deterioration in health. At a high level of infestation, they may be seen in the fecal matter, but normally it will require fecal microscopy by your vet. This will establish the species and the relative density of the eggs, thus the level of infestation.

Treatment is normally via tablets, but liquids are also available. Because worms are so common, the best husbandry technique is to routinely treat breeding cats for worms prior to their being bred, then for the queen and her kittens to be treated periodically. Discuss a testing and treatment program with your vet.

NEUTERING AND SPAYING

Desexing your cat is normally done when a female is about four months of age and somewhat later with a male. The operation is quite simple with a male but more complicated with a female. It is still a routine procedure. It is possible to delay estrus in a breeding queen, but the risk of negative side effects makes this a dubious course to take. Discuss it with your vet. A cat of any age can be neutered (male) or spayed (female); but if they are adults, they take some months (especially males) before they lose their old habits.

Given routine care, the Fold's ears are no more susceptible to ear mites and other ear-related problems than are those of erect-eared cats.

FIRST AID

Although you might think that such inquisitive creatures as cats would be prone to many physical injuries, this is not actually the case. They usually extricate themselves from dangerous situations because of their very fast reflexes. However, injuries do happen, and the most common is caused by the cat darting across a road and being hit by a vehicle. About 10 percent of cats die annually due to traffic accidents. The next level of injury will be caused by cats getting bitten or scratched when fighting among themselves, or being bitten by an insect, or by a sharp object getting lodged in their fur or feet.

If your cat is hit by a vehicle, the first thing to do is to try and place it on a board of some sort and remove it to a safe place. Do not lift its head because this might result in it swallowing blood into the lungs. Try to keep it calm by talking soothingly to it.

If the cat is still mobile, but has clearly been badly hurt, you must try and restrict its movements by wrapping it in a blanket or towel. If it is bleeding badly, try to contain the flow by wrapping a bandage around the body or leg to reduce the blood loss. With a minor cut, you should trim the hair away from the wound, bathe it, then apply an antiseptic or stem the flow with a styptic pencil or other coagulant.

If you suspect that your cat has been bitten by an insect and the result is a swelling, the poison is already in the skin so external ointments will have virtually no effect. The same is true of an abscess caused by fighting. The only answer is to let your vet use surgery to lance and treat the wound.

Fortunately, cats rarely swallow poison because they are such careful eaters. In all instances, immediately contact your vet and advise him of the kind of poison the cat has consumed.

If your cat should ever be badly frightened, for example, by a dog chasing and maybe biting it, the effect of this may not be apparent immediately. It may go into shock some time later. Keep the cat indoors so that you can see how it reacts. Should it go into shock and collapse, place a blanket around it and take it to the vet. If this is not possible, place it in a darkened room and cover it with a blanket so it does not lose too much body heat. Comfort it until you can make contact with the vet.

Following the basics of good husbandry will go a long way in helping to keep your Scottish Fold in good health.

EXHIBITING SCOTTISH FOLDS

From the first time cats were seriously exhibited in London in 1871, the cat show has been the very heart of the fancy. It is the place where breeders can have the merits of their stock assessed in a competitive framework, where all cat lovers can meet and discuss ideas, trends and needs, and where new products for cats can be promoted. It is the only event in which you have the opportunity of seeing just about every color and pattern variety that exists in the Scottish Fold breed.

Even if you have no plans to become a breeder or exhibitor, you should visit at least one or two cat shows to see what a quality Scottish Fold looks like.

TYPES OF SHOW

Shows range from the small informal affairs that attract a largely local entry to the major all-breed championships and specialty exhibitions that can be spread over two or more days (but only one in Britain). A specialty is a show restricted either by breed or by hair length (short or long). In the US, it is quite common for two or more shows to run concurrently at the same site.

SHOW CLASSES

The number of classes staged at a given show will obviously reflect its size, but the classes fall into various major divisions. These are championships for whole cats, premierships for altered cats, open classes for both of the previous cats, kittens, and household pets. In all but the pet class, there are separate classes for males and females. There are then classes for all of the color and pattern varieties. At a small show, the color/patterns may be grouped into fewer classes than at a major show.

All classes are judged against the standard for the breed, other than pet classes, in which the exhibits are judged on the basis of condition and general appeal, or uniqueness of pattern. An unregistered Scottish Fold can be entered into a pet class, and it will be judged on the same basis as would a mixed breed. A kitten in the US is a cat of four months of age but under eight months on the day of a show. In Britain a kitten is a cat of three or more months and under nine months on the show day.

AWARDS AND PRIZES

The major awards in cats are those of Champion and Grand Champion, Premier and Grand Premier. In Britain, a cat must win three challenge certificates under different judges to become a champion, while in the US it must win six winner's ribbons. In both instances, these awards are won via the open class. Once a cat is a champion, it then competes in the champions' class and becomes a grand based on points earned in defeating other champions. The prizes can range from certificates, ribbons and cups to trophies and cash.

Wins in kitten classes do not count toward champion status. Champion status in one association does not carry over to another, in which a cat would have to win its title again based on the rules of that association. The rules of competition are complex, and any would-be exhibitor should obtain a copy of them from their particular registry.

The general format of cat shows, while differing somewhat from one country to another, is much the same in broad terms. A Scottish Fold will enter its color or pattern class. If it wins, it will progress to compete against other group winners in its breed, and ultimately compete for best of breed. If classes have been scheduled for all of the recognized colors and patterns in all of the recognized breeds, then a Best in Show will be the ultimate award. The Best in Show (BIS) award is the highest honor that a cat can receive and the dream of every cat exhibitor.

JUDGING

As stated earlier, cats are judged against their written standard rather than against each other. A winning cat is one that records the highest total of points, or, put another way, the least number of demerit marks. In the US cats are taken to the judge's table for assessment, but in Britain the judge moves around the pens with a trolley. In the US, judging is done in front of the public, but in the UK judging is normally done before the public is allowed into the hall. The exhibit owners are requested to leave the hall during judging.

CAT PENS

When you arrive at the cat show, a pen will be allocated to your cat. This is an all-wire cage. In Britain, the rules governing what can be placed into the cage are very rigid. This is because there can be no means of identifying the owner of the cat when the judge arrives at that pen. Thus, the blanket, the litter box and the water vessel must all be white. In the US the pens are highly decorated with silks, gorgeous cushions, and so on because the cat is taken to another pen for judging.

THE EXHIBITION SCOTTISH FOLD

Obviously, a Scottish Fold show cat must be a very sound example of its breed. Its coat must be in truly beautiful condition because the level of competition is extremely high at the major events. At more local affairs, the quality will not be as high, which gives more exhibitors a chance to pick up victories in the absence of the top cats of the country. The male cat must have two descended testicles and have a valid vaccination certificate against feline enteritis that was issued at least seven days before the show. It should have tested

A Scottish Fold show cat must be a very good specimen of its breed. Flaws that may be seen in pet-quality Scottish Folds will not be present in the exhibition Scottish Fold.

negative for feline leukemia (and/or any other diseases as required by your registry).

A show cat must be well-mannered because if it should bite or claw the judge, it is hardly likely to win favor. It could even be disqualified, depending on the regulations of your registry. In any case, such a cat could not be examined properly by the judge, so this alone would preclude it from any hope of winning. It must therefore become accustomed to such treatment by being handled very often as a kitten by friends and relatives.

ENTERING A SHOW

You must apply to the show secretary for an entry blank and a schedule. The secretary will list the classes and state the rules of that association. The entry form must be completed and returned, with fees due, by the last date of entry as stipulated for that show. It is very important that you enter the correct classes; otherwise, your cat will be eliminated and your fee forfeited. If you are unsure about this aspect, you can seek the advice of an exhibitor of your acquaintance, or simply call the

show secretary, who will advise you.

SHOW ITEMS

When attending a show you will need a variety of items. They include a cat carrier, litter box, blankets, food and water vessels, food, your cat's own supply of your local water if necessary, disinfectant, first aid kit, grooming tools, paper towels, entry pass, vaccination certificates, show catalog to check the entry for your cat and when it is likely to be judged, a small stool, and decorations for the pen. You may also wish to take your own food. Indeed, it would be wise to invest in a collapsible

Good body study of a red tabby and white Fold. Note the long, tapered tail. Owner, Gwen Hornung.

cart or trolley to transport all of the above!

The best advice is that you should visit shows and talk with exhibitors so that you can get the feel of things before you make the plunge yourself. Showing is a fascinating and thoroughly addictive pastime, but it is also time-consuming, can be costly, and entails a great deal of dedication. Fortunately, you can participate to whatever level you wish. You are also assured of making many new friends in the process.